Otters Love to Play

Jonathan London

illustrated by **Meilo So**

CANDLEWICK PRESS

Is that a beaver lodge?

No!

Last year beavers made their home there,
but this year it's . . .

an OTTER DEN!

Otters often use dens abandoned by beavers, muskrats, or woodchucks — with an aboveground entrance added. Otters are members of the weasel family, which includes weasels, badgers, and wolverines.

It's spring, and in a nest of moss, leaves, and grass, three newborn otter babies drink warm rich milk at their mother's teats.

Baby otters are called pups or cubs. They're born blind and toothless and weigh around two ounces (55 grams) — about the size of a small candy bar. They nurse for four months.

4

At five weeks old, they open their eyes for the first time!

THEY CAN SEE!

Female otters give birth to babies at two years old and have anywhere from one to six pups in a litter. The mother otter chases her mate away when the pups are born.

In another month, the pups' mother
lets them out of the den to play.

OTTERS LOVE TO PLAY!

They leap and tumble and pounce on one another.
They chew on ears and wrestle and roll.

They chase and play tag and race.

Two pups grab the ends of a stick—
it's an otter tug-of-war!

Playing is fun, but otters play with a purpose. For young otters, play helps them to develop the speed and agility needed for hunting. And for all otters, playing strengthens family ties.

And now that the pups' furry coats are grown in and waterproof, let the swimming lessons begin!

The otters' mother carries the pups by the scruff of their necks to the riverbank and drops them in.

Ka-Splash!

11

Being in the water is fun, and the otters' mother
gives the pups a ride down the river on her back.

Then she teaches them how to swim!
She supports them to the surface, and they follow
her in single file and do what she does.

An otter has webbed feet and kicks with its hind legs, using its powerful tail as a rudder. Otters are graceful underwater and can swim seven miles (eleven kilometers) per hour — faster than an Olympic swimmer!

Within days,
the otter pups
gracefully spin
and flip
and swish
like underwater
acrobats.

They scramble up a mud slide and
SLIIIIIIIIIIDE back down to the water—

Ka-Splash!

And they do it again and again!

By the end of summer, the otters' mother has taught the pups how to catch small fish with their sharp teeth and poke among the rocks and in the mud for frogs, crayfish, turtles, and snakes.

Otters' whiskers are long and sensitive. They use them to feel along the bottom and inside cracks in rocks, searching for food. Otters' main food is fish, and they can eat a quarter of their body weight in a single day.

Now the leaves turn colors and start to fall,
and already the otter pups are almost full grown.

When otters aren't busy frolicking or hunting, they scent-mark the area near home to warn intruders away.

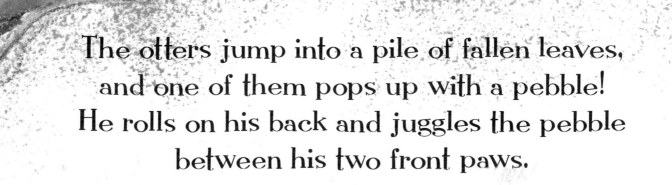

The otters jump into a pile of fallen leaves,
and one of them pops up with a pebble!
He rolls on his back and juggles the pebble
between his two front paws.

The days grow shorter, the nights
grow longer, and one day, winter
blows in with a blast of white.

But winter doesn't slow otters down.
The pups' fur is thick and warm—

and it's playtime again!

Otters have dense fur with protective guard hairs and produce an oil that keeps their skin dry. They keep their fur's protective qualities by grooming themselves, which they do by rolling on the ground or in the snow or rubbing against logs.

The pups belly-slide down a snowbank . . .
but wait!

What's that?

Something's waiting.
Something's watching.

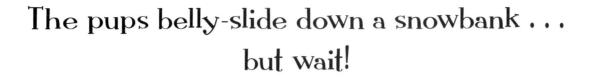

Mother otters are known for their fierce defense of their young, which are prey to foxes, owls, bobcats, lynxes, and in some places, wolves. Full-grown otters can run and slide on snow at up to 18 miles (29 kilometers) per hour.

IT'S A FOX!

The otters' mother SCREAMS,
hunches up,
slides across the snow,
and with a terrible GRRRROWL . . .

scares the fox away!

Throughout the winter, the otter family
snuggles in a ball of fur in the den.

And when they are hungry,
they dive in icy water for fish.

Otters don't hibernate. And throughout winter, the pups continue to grow.
Full-grown females may weigh 11 to 22 pounds (5 to 10 kilograms), males as much as 32 pounds (14 kilograms).

And when spring
comes, the year-old pups
emerge from the den and
speed down the mud slide—

SWIIIIIIIIIIIISH!

Why? . . .

BECAUSE OTTERS LOVE TO PLAY!

INDEX

Look up the pages to find out all about these otter things.
Don't forget to look at both kinds of words: this kind and this kind.

ABOUT OTTERS

Otters are the most playful creatures of all wildlife. There are thirteen species of otters; the ones in this story are North American river otters. This species was once commonly hunted and trapped for its thick, warm fur; now the biggest threats these otters face are water pollution and loss of habitat. They share many similarities with European river otters, which had been experiencing a severe population decline but, thanks to conservation efforts, are now making a strong comeback. Though some European river otters live along the coast of Norway, they are not to be confused with true sea otters of the North Pacific coast. Other species include African clawless otters, Asian small-clawed otters — which are the smallest species of otter — and giant otters, which are as long as a man is tall! There is even a hairy-nosed otter. But one thing all otters have in common is . . . they all love to play!

For Sean, Steph, Leah, Claire,
Michael & sweet Maureen
J. L.

For Peter the Cellist
M. S.

First edition 2016

Library of Congress Catalog Card Number 2015933247
ISBN 978-0-7636-6913-3

15 16 17 18 19 20 TWP 10 9 8 7 6 5 4 3 2 1

Printed in Johor Bahru, Malaysia

This book was typeset in Malonia Voigo and Myriad Pro.
The illustrations were done in watercolor.

Candlewick Press
99 Dover Street
Somerville, Massachusetts 02144

visit us at www.candlewick.com